W9-ALD-959

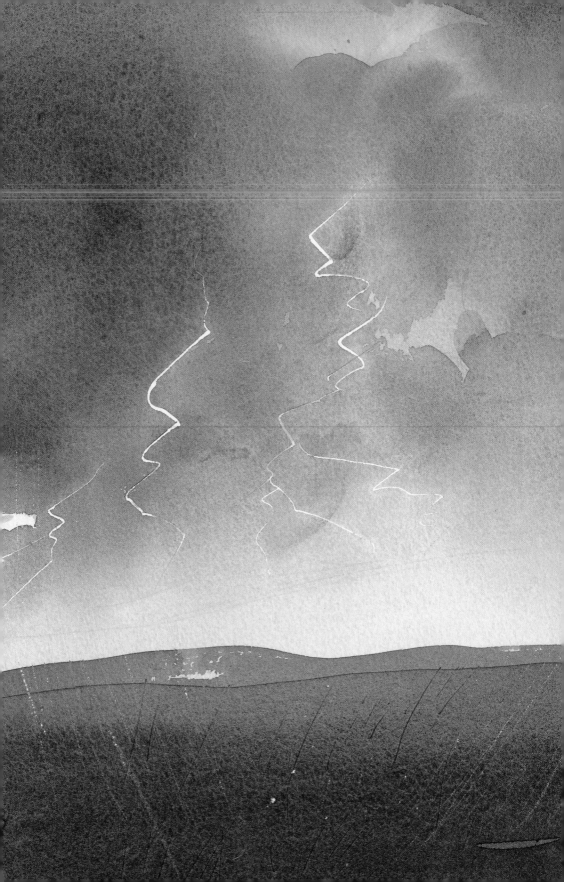

In memory of Alfred Meaden – BB

For all those with the spirit of adventure – RBC

First edition for the United States
published by Barron's Educational Series, Inc., 1996.

First published in Great Britain in 1995 by
Gollancz Children's Paperbacks;
A Division of the Cassell Group
Wellington House
125 Strand
London WC2R 0BB

Produced by Mathew Price Ltd.
The Old Glove Factory
Bristol Road
Sherborne
Dorset DT9 4HP

Text copyright © 1995 by Beverley Birch
Illustrations copyright © 1995 by Robin Bell Corfield

Designed by Herman Lelie

All rights reserved.

No part of this book may be reproduced in
any form, by photostat, microfilm, xerography, or any other
means, or incorporated into any information retrieval system,
electronic or mechanical, without the written permission of the
copyright owner.

All inquiries should be addressed to:
Barron's Educational Series, Inc.
250 Wireless Boulevard
Hauppauge, New York 11788

Library of Congress Catalog Card No. 96-83303

ISBN 0-8120-6622-7 (hardcover)
    0-8120-9790-4 (paperback)

Printed in Hong Kong
987654321

BENJAMIN FRANKLIN'S

ADVENTURES WITH ELECTRICITY

Beverley Birch
Illustrated by Robin Bell Corfield

Lightning forked across the sky, flaring with a sudden brilliance into the darkening afternoon. Benjamin Franklin rose from his desk, and moved to the window to watch.

He saw each detail of the lightning's path—its crooked flame across the sky, its fierce white light, and then its deafening crack like the heavens exploding.

Franklin thought of how it could kill an animal or a person at a stroke, or split a large tree into splinters. How it could blast the steeple off a church into a thousand pieces, and run along metal like fire, melting it to a flaming liquid.

Even bell ringers, climbing towers to send out a storm warning, had died from its fiery stroke. And Franklin thought of the stench of burning, and the charred ashes left by the lightning's strike.

So much like the hissing, crackling sparks he made here in his own home, with glass tubes and whirling globes!

He thought of all the experiments he had done since he was first spellbound by the sparking force developed from a glass tube.

And he remembered the day, years ago,
when he and his friends first saw that spark. In
the hands of the visiting scientist, it seemed
like magic—a young boy, hung from the
ceiling on silk threads, and the scientist merely
rubbed a glass tube in his hands as he held it
near the boy's feet. The boy's hair stood up
and sparks flew from his nose and hands—
long sparks that snapped toward your
knuckles!

Franklin remembered coming home, filled with excitement and curiosity, to try it himself. First, by rubbing a glass tube, and watching the spark flare with a fierce crackle as he put his hand close.

His friends, too, came to watch and to try it themselves. They learned how to lead the force along a wire into a glass bottle, and collect it there. They learned to lead the force out again, when they wanted to.

They passed sparks between each other. Handshakes, kisses, standing on the floor, or on wooden stands or blocks of wax—one person on the wax and one on the floor.

Hours, weeks, months were filled with them trying everything they could think of. And such long letters they wrote to each other about it all—one trying an idea and passing it on to the next; the next trying and sending back his thoughts. Each idea building on the one before.

As their amazement grew, they had glass globes made with a handle to turn it, and a pad set to rub the surface of the globe as it spun.

The rubbed glass could pass its strange sparking force into a hundred different things—a cannon ball, a gun barrel, a crowbar, knitting needles, fire tongs and a poker, a bullet, some chains, a tea kettle (filled with water and empty), wood, bricks, water, chalk, salt—even the gilt paint on a mirror, or the gold flowers painted on a china cup.

They saw, too, another puzzling thing. When objects had the strange force in them, they would sometimes draw other things toward them, and sometimes push them away. If they took up one of the objects and held it as they walked around the room, a feather or a piece of fluff would float ahead, as if an invisible hand was thrusting it away.

Some things seemed to hold the force and refuse to pass it on. If you stood anything on a block of wax, the sparking force would go no further, but stop at the wax itself.

And it was the same with silk thread. If you hung something like a gun barrel from the ceiling on silk thread, any force that flowed from the glass globe into the gun barrel would stay there.

But if you hung the same gun barrel on copper wire, the force ran straight up the copper wire and away into the roof beams.

Some other materials, such as wet things and all sorts of metal, also passed the force on in an instant. A sharp metal point held as much as eight inches away could draw the force off at once and pass it on to your hand —with a great shock to the hand, and a loud noise!

Once, Franklin sent the force running like a bright flame through the gilded binding of a book! He melted brass pins and needles. He punched holes through thick board, as though it was the thinnest paper. He set dry gun powder on fire.

Sometimes the force leaped through the air in a snapping brush of blue flame. Sometimes it was a short, fierce spark.

But it always reminded him of the blinding light and the crooked flash of lightning.

Like lightning, his glass globe's spark could also kill an animal by shock or by burning. And when it burned, it left the same stench of charred remains. The more Franklin thought about it, the more he wanted to develop his ideas for his friends to read. All his ideas were very, very new.

This all happened in the mid-1700s, long before electricity ran in wires in people's homes. All that people understood about electricity was that there were strange sparks and crackling noises if you rubbed certain materials such as glass. They knew the rubbed materials would attract light objects like hair or fluff, or push them away. This sparking force was named *electricity,* and they knew that it gave off a prickling feeling. Sometimes it gave a fierce jolt that was strong enough to stun a person, or leave one feeling weak for hours.

But they knew no more than that. They could not use the spark to light or warm their homes, or to run machines, or to send messages. It was a fascinating mystery, but they had no use for it.

And Franklin's thoughts always returned to one particular puzzle in the mystery of the electric spark: How much his small spark was like a tiny cousin of the fearful flame of destruction in the sky—a bolt of lightning!

A little spark and a big spark. A small flow of electricity and a large flow of electricity.

Franklin was certain they were the same. They looked alike, they sounded alike, they could both burn and melt and destroy. But could you attract lightning onto a metal point, the way you could attract the spark from a glass globe onto the point of a needle?

Could you lead lightning down a wire into a bottle? And could you then do all the other things you could do with the electricity that flowed from a glass globe? He had already worked out a way of finding out, and had written it down for others to try.

This was his plan: Raise a long iron rod high on a tower or steeple. Give the rod a sharp point at the top, and fasten its bottom end into a stand in a sort of sentry box below, where a person could watch while sheltered from the rain. From there, the person could find out if lightning from the clouds did flow down the rod, by seeing if sparks could be drawn from it.

But Franklin hadn't tried it himself, and in the end his idea had to be tested. This was how all their ideas had grown—passed on in letters written to friends and letters they wrote back, so that their knowledge grew, built up trial by trial, like bricks in a building.

The problem was that his lightning plan needed a high building, and in Philadelphia, where he lived, there was no building tall enough to take his iron rod up into the sky.

Hot weather was coming. Storms were brewing, he could feel it.

Franklin had two reasons for wanting to know if he was right about the lightning—the wonderful strangeness of it, and the usefulness of it. For, if he was right, he could see a way to lead lightning safely into the ground—and then how many people, animals, and homes might be saved from that deadly stroke?

Yet the problem remained. There was no building high enough, and yet a sharp metal point must somehow be carried into the sky, to attract the lightning.

The problem nagged at him. How could he get it high enough? How could he hold it there?

It must go high.

He had a sudden vision of children flying kites on windy hills, of kites soaring as high as the strings would let them.

Kites!

But then he imagined a paper kite tearing in the wet gusts of a storm.

No, he would need a material that could hold against the battering of wind and rain, something that would support his iron rod, but not steal the electricity from it, something that electricity would not easily run through. Like the silk threads he used in his other experiments. Silk.

He found a silk handkerchief. It was big and square enough, but it needed a frame—light and strong. He thought about that for a while, and then got to work. Under his busy hands the shape began to form—a simple wooden cross, each arm long enough to reach the four corners of the handkerchief.

Next, a tail, so that the kite would fly well in the air. And a long string to hold it by. Then he came to the rod.

The rod could not be too heavy or it would drag the kite to the ground. Thin wire, perhaps? And sharpened to a fine point, because he had found that a point attracted electricity much better than a round or a blunt end.

If he was right, the lightning electricity would flow down the rod, and into the string. But there must be something at the other end of the string, to stop the electricity from flowing on.

Silk again.

He found a silk ribbon and tied it on. Now he could hold that in his hand, and it would not let the lightning pass from the string into his hand.

He had reached the final part of his design.
Where the silk ribbon joined the string, he
fastened a metal key. The electricity would
flow easily from the string into the key, but
there it would stop because it would not go
through the silk.

So now Franklin had a new plan. He would fly the kite when storm clouds gathered. He feared that electricity might be able to run through a wet silk ribbon, so he would shelter himself and the ribbon from rain.

If he was right, and if he had arranged everything properly, the wire would draw the electricity from the thunder clouds. Electricity would flow into the string and on down, down, to the key at the end.

And there, from the metal key, he should be able to draw sparks.

The weather grew hotter. He strolled out into the fields looking for the right place—not too far from his house, open enough to raise the kite without tangling it in trees, and with a shed for shelter. He told his twenty-one-year-old son William about his kite plan, for he would need help. But he told no one else. If it worked he would tell; if it failed, he would just have to try something else.

The summer moved on. It was hot and damp, getting hotter every day until it seemed to steam. He searched the sky for the rain-filled clouds he needed.

Then one day he heard the thunder rumbling.
In the far distance, dark clouds gathered.
Franklin called his son.

Up into the swelling winds the kite swooped, lifting its iron point toward the dark rain clouds.

Backing into the shelter, out of the rain and wind, Franklin grasped the silk ribbon. The string must not touch the door frame, or the electricity might leak away and never reach the key.

A large cloud passed overhead, black with rain. Lightning flashed, died, flashed again, and for a moment the world was lit with its white flickering. But on the string and on the key nothing changed.

Minutes passed—a quarter of an hour, half an hour. Rain streamed off the grassy mounds in the field, and the mud sucked at their feet.

Franklin gripped the silk ribbon even more firmly. It was taking so long, he began to wonder if it was hopeless waiting any longer. But he must do the experiment properly, and stay until the end of the storm if he had to.

There was a sudden
coolness on his hand. He could feel the gentle
stroking of a light wind across his skin, like
someone's breath. In the near darkness he saw
that loose threads of the string were moving.

They were standing straight out from the
downward line of the string.

Standing away from each other!

He had seen it happen before, on string
electrified with the glass globe. Loose fibers of
the string always pushed each other away.

Eagerly but slowly, carefully, he put his free hand out, knuckle first. He edged it toward the metal key.

The string fibers moved.

Closer with his knuckle. . .

The fibers sprang outward, stiff, with a short, fierce spark!

He pulled his hand back.

Again, knuckle out, advancing slowly, nearer, nearer...

A vast crackling and popping and hissing —and electricity streamed through the wet air.

Franklin gave swift instructions to his son: one after the other the glass jars were to be brought, and each jar was to be charged with electricity from the key.

For now came the second part of his plan. He must find out if this lightning was the same sparking force he knew as electricity. Could it really do all the things he had done with the electricity from his whirling glass globes?

Franklin knew the answers, even as they packed the jars for the return home, even though he knew he would do each test as carefully as he had ever done it, just to make sure before he wrote it all down for his friends to read.

The glass globe spark was a small electrical flow through the air. The lightning spark was a big electrical flow through the air. The cloud was like a big jar, collecting electricity, and his kite wire had led it out.
He had proved it, with his kite experiment.

It might have killed him. Now, we know it was a miracle that it didn't.

Franklin did not realize the danger of what he had just done. No one fully understood it yet, but they would soon find out—for a scientist did die while testing Franklin's ideas. He had incorrectly arranged his equipment and led the lightning straight into his own body. The shock was so violent that his heart stopped.

Perhaps, if Franklin had waited any longer before he led the electricity into the jars— holding a silk ribbon that became wetter and wetter, until it was soaked and the electricity could run through to his hand—perhaps. . .

Instead, Franklin ran safely home. Already the next plan was taking shape in his mind. He was picturing a metal point, set on top of buildings or ships' masts, ready to draw lightning out of the clouds and lead it safely down the outside of a building or ship into the ground or the water. No harm would come to any person, home, or animal.

Franklin's busy brain was already giving birth to the first lightning rod.

Today we use electricity to light and heat our homes. Electricity powers our machines—from ovens, food mixers, and electric drills, to vast machines in factories. It controls hospital equipment, traffic lights, telephones, and computers. It is hard to imagine life without it.

When Benjamin Franklin was learning about electricity, however, people had no idea how it could be used. It was a mysterious force that sparked and crackled in interesting (and frightening) ways.

But Franklin's work was very important in the story of electricity. Even before he became famous for his kite experiment in 1752, he discovered new things about how the strange force behaved. Within 70 years his work led other scientists to take Franklin's discoveries, add to them, and so give us the first electrical inventions.

When Franklin was working in the 1750s, electricity was still only a scientific game. His lightning rod was the first and only real use for the knowledge. Scientists did not yet know how to make electricity flow continuously.

It took 48 more years before someone learned that. Alessandro Volta invented the electric battery in 1800, in Italy. An electric battery creates a continuous flow of electricity—an electric current. From then on, scientists in many different countries began to make discoveries very quickly. By 1837 electricity could be used to send messages by telegraph, and within 10 more years scientists began to develop the first electric light. By the 1870s scientists and inventors were discovering new ways to use electricity almost every year.

The age of electricity had begun.

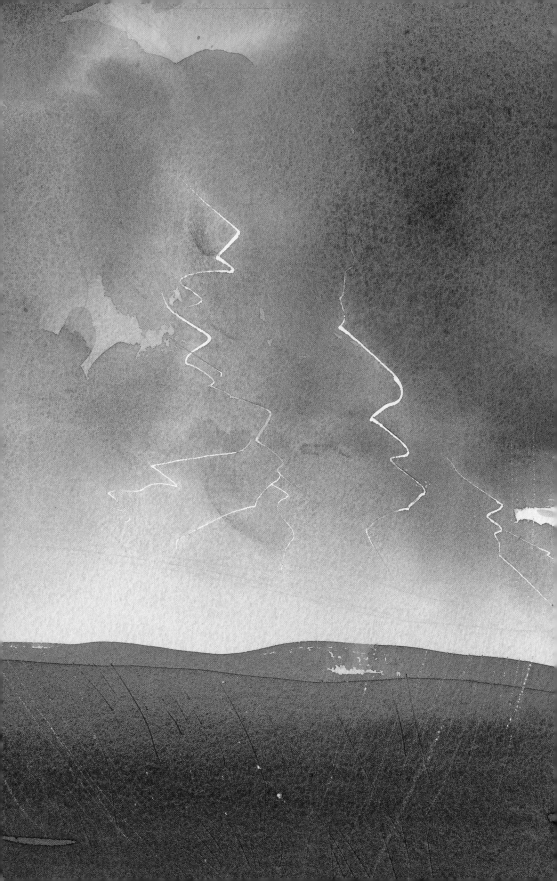

The Science Stories Books
by Beverley Birch

Benjamin Franklin's Adventures with Electricity
Illustrated by Robin Bell Corfield

Marconi's Battle for Radio
Illustrated by Robin Bell Corfield

Marie Curie's Search for Radium
Illustrated by Christian Birmingham

Pasteur's Fight against Microbes
Illustrated by Christian Birmingham